Contents

Given the chance, field gladiolus *(Gladiolus italicus)* quickly colonises cultivated land. Gladioli are seen here with common asphodel *(Asphodelus aestivus)* which has also benefitted from man-made changes that keep competing vegetation in check.

What Makes the Algarve so Special?

The common poppy *(Papaver rhoeas)* blooms in March and April in the Algarve.

Visit southern Portugal in the early part of the year and you see wildflowers everywhere. From January through to May there is hardly a piece of ground, no matter how small, that does not have its own colourful display. Later, when the temperature soars, it is hard to believe that such a fabulous riot of colour preceded the brown, dried-up vegetation that dominates the summer landscape.

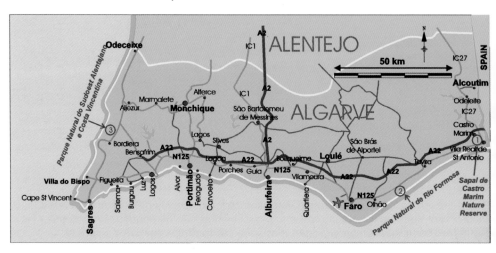

For those of us old enough to have known the countryside of Britain and northern Europe half a century ago, scenes like many shown in this book replay experiences from our childhood: cornfields flushed with poppies and cornflowers; butterfly meadows peppered with wild orchids; and waysides where wildflowers smother banks, hedges and ditches. In the Algarve of today, farming still relies much more on sunshine than on the herbicides, insecticides and artificial fertilisers that have stolen so much of our own countryside colour. Organic rather than intensive farming is practised across much of the Mediterranean region. As a result the region is home to more than 10,000 species of flowering plants - mostly native ones, but with a fair number of introduced plants thriving alongside them.

That's not to say time has stood still in Portugal, but many of the land-use changes here have been good for the native plants. Even the cutting of roadside verges to reduce fire risk in summer favours some of the less robust wildflowers – wild orchids in particular. Of course, farming inevitably causes some plants to become marginalised, restricted to places that people and farm animals find inaccessible, but it also creates new habitats in which other wildflowers flourish where they might not otherwise have done. Welcome *back*, therefore, to the wildflower-rich lands of the Algarve!

Large Blue Alkanet *(Anchusa azurea)* is a common wayside plant in the Algarve.

Tourists flock to the Algarve for its wonderful weather and natural environment. Ironically, development to meet the growing demand for villas, hotels and golf courses consumes the precious land and water resources that are the Algarve's source of wealth. (Many Portuguese rivers now dry up completely in summer.) Recognising the need to balance development with the preservation of the natural landscape, the Portuguese authorities have designated some of the most beautiful wild places as National Parks. (See pages 63 - 65).

Algarve Wildflower Habitats

Although its coast faces the Atlantic Ocean, the Algarve shares the wet, mild winters and hot dry summers - sometimes up to five months without rain - that characterise Mediterranean-climate regions in other parts of the world. Perhaps surprisingly, this climate is not restricted to those countries bordering the Mediterranean Sea: in North and South America, the Cape area of South Africa and in southern Australia there are Mediterranean-climate regions sharing this unique weather pattern and with distinctive plant communities adapted to the climatic conditions. The collective size of these regions, at a mere two percent of our planet's land surface, is no measure of its importance in terms of flora and fauna. This small area contains some 20 per cent of the plant species known to mankind.

Bush and forest fires are an all-too-frequent feature of Algarve summers, and indeed fire has had a major influence on wildflower evolution here. Species with the ability to regenerate from root systems or from bulbs protected below ground from the ravages of the summer blazes do well. In fact some of the plants actually depend on fire to penetrate their specially toughened seed cases, releasing the seeds and stimulating them to grow and flower.

While the Algarve and other Mediterranean regions provide ideal conditions for plants, they are also places where people like to live. Over thousands of years Man has cleared most of the accessible land of its original tree cover to create open areas either for grazing animals or for growing arable crops, grapes, oranges, almonds, olives, figs and so on. The land-use regime has, in turn, determined which wildflowers now grow in abundance here.

Thyme broomrape *(Orobanche alba),* a parasite on thyme plants and related species, is a very common sight on fallowed agricultural land throughout the Algarve.

Wildflower Hotspots

You can find Algarve wildflowers in the littoral zone (the coastal cliffs and coves); in forested mountainous regions (known as the 'serra'); along river valleys; and in the maquis (areas with moderate rainfall that support shrubs up to about five metres tall) and the garrigue (drier habitats up to about 50 metres above sea level comprising compact cushions of plants and shrubs with bare stony areas in between that make the going fairly easy underfoot). From December through to June these are all places where plenty of wildflowers bloom.

A tangle of wildflowers on the cliffs near Carvoeiro

But if you have only a limited amount of time available and you want to see lots of wildflowers, concentrate on the garrigue, the zone that lies between the coastal strip and the wooded hills further inland. This narrow strip of land is home to a vast array of plants – indeed, many of the wild orchids for which the Algarve is renowned can be found there.

Barbary nut *(Gynandriris sisyrinchium)*, an iris-like wildflower, blooms on the Algarve from late January onwards. The short-lived flowers open in mid afternoon and close again as dusk descends.

How to Use this Book

Rather than a formal identification guide this book is a celebration of the beauty of the Algarve and its wonderful wildflowers - a souvenir of the wonderful floral sites (and sights) you can expect to come across if you are on holiday when the Algarve is 'in bloom'. We hope that it will help you to find, enjoy and identify many of the lovely flowers that are commonplace as well as a few unusual ones you may come across in Southern Portugal.

Most of us see wildflowers as an aside to whatever we are doing when on holiday. For that reason we have divided this book into sections covering the kinds of plants you could expect to see when driving or walking along roadsides, visiting some of the beautiful cliffs and coves, strolling beside a lake or a stream, or taking a trip to the mountains and woodlands that lie beyond the beaches and towns where most of us stay when in the Algarve. Certain plants can be found only by water, or in woodland or high in the hills. However, categorising wildflowers by their preferred habitats provides only a rough guide to locating particular species, because many of the plants bloom in more than one kind of habitat, appearing earlier in the lowlands and rather later in the cooler air of higher altitudes.

The huge diversity of Algarve wildflowers makes it difficult to settle on a shortlist of just a few dozen species. Some common wildflowers are inconspicuous and rarely seen, and so we have concentrated on those more likely to catch the eye - flowers that jump out at you and insist that you try to find out what they are.

Colours make flowers memorable. We have therefore included wildflower 'galleries' at the back of major sections and, wherever practicable, arranged their contents by colour, starting with white and progressing through yellow, red and purple through to blue.

At the back of the book is a list of National Parks and Nature Reserves in the Algarve, with details of the terrain and the kinds of plants you can expect to see. Home to many lovely wildflowers, these reserves are also havens for numerous birds, insects and other animals.

Garrigue habitat with its hiker-friendly gaps between the low-growing shrubs and pincushions of wildflowers

By the Way

Spring flights to the Algarve that arrive after dark should be banned: to miss the displays of wayside flowers that greet us is to lose out on one of the highlights of a visit to Portugal.

Many flowers that we regard as garden plants and pay a lot of money for in garden centres and nurseries grow beside roads and on rough ground in the Algarve - gladiolus, Hottentot fig, cistus, lupin, borage and arum lily to name but a few. These plants are a very good guide to what will do well in an Algarve garden, whereas the battle to sustain an 'English rose garden' in the blistering heat of southern Portugal is one lost by all but those able to keep up the daily watering regime necessary for survival of drought-intolerant plants.

Urbanisation is bad news for plants that require undisturbed habitats, but it helps others that need cultivation to trigger germination. Many new-villa owners find that their gardening work produces less colourful results than Nature's efforts on the to-be-developed plot near their new houses, as the picture below of a recent development at Burgau shows.

There is no doubt that, once the spring rains cease, gardening in the Algarve has its disadvantages - something that many more of us may come to experience as global warming brings the southern-Europe climate further north. Fortunately, once plants get established beside highways and byways (and this includes cultivated flowers as well as wild ones) they are often ready to exploit any opportunity available to them in order to continue to exist. Several of the Algarve's wild orchids, including the mirror orchid *(Ophrys speculum* – see page 12*)* and the yellow ophrys *(Ophrys lutea* - see page 24*)* can also be found beside busy roads.

Damaged blades of this prickly pear *(Opuntia ficus-indica)* provide convenient homes for geraniums that would otherwise have died from lack of water after the garden where they were originally planted was abandoned. (Inset: flower of the Prickly Pear).

On a roof well out of harm's way, and free from the need to compete with more vigorous deep-rooting plants, wall pennywort *(Umbilicus rupestris)*, an early-flowering member of the stonecrop family, is flourishing in a very dry situation.

The mirror orchid *(Ophrys speculum)*, one of the most common of the Algarve's wild orchids, is often seen on roadsides and beside footpaths between March and May.

Dutchman's pipe *(Aristolochia baetica)* is another common sight on the roadsides of Portugal, where it scrambles over walls, fences and other plants.

Hollow-stemmed Asphodel
(Asphodelus fistulosus)
February to June

A smaller plant than common asphodel (see page 38), this is a very common wayside wildflower in the Algarve. Hollow-stemmed asphodel (also known as hollow-leaved asphodel) can, as the name suggests, be distinguished from its more robust relative by its hollow, cylindrical leaves.

Ramping Fumitory
(Fumaria capreolata)
March to June

Very common on roadsides and in damp ditches, ramping fumitory does rather as its name suggests: it spreads far and wide, frequently scrambling over other plants growing in the same places.

Crown Daisy
(Chrysanthemum coronarium)
March to September

Probably the best-known wildflower in the Algarve and much loved by everybody. It is difficult to categorise it to one particular habitat type as the crown daisy is found throughout the Algarve on waysides, wasteland, fallow farmland, by the sea – anywhere, really!

European Umbrella Milkwort
(Tolpis barbata)
March to May

Unrelated to the tiny blue milkwort flowers (*Polygala* species) of close-cropped pastures in northern Europe, this member of the daisy family (Asteraceae) is found throughout the Algarve on disturbed land.

Andryala
(Andryala integrifolia)
April to July

The height of this very hairy plant varies considerably: the specimen pictured here was exceptionally tall. It has delightful pale lemon flowers and favours dry, rocky places.

Bladder Vetch
(Anthyllis tetraphylla)
March to June

This plant forms large, spreading colonies on waysides, fallow farmland and throughout the garrigue generally. The pretty yellow and white flowers give way to fruits that become greatly enlarged – hence its common name.

15

Yellow Chamomile
(Anthemis tinctoria)
May to August

Yellow chamomile forms large and rather 'leggy' plant colonies throughout the Algarve, appearing on waysides and in other low-lying places.

Grey-leaved Cistus
(Cistus albidus)
February to June

One of many cistus shrubs that flourish in the Algarve, this one has lovely large, pink flowers with fragile-looking petals that seem, upon close inspection, to be thoroughly creased. It is found on waysides in both garrigue and maquis habitats as well as in open woodlands.

Common Mallow
(Malva neglecta)
April to September

Also referred to as dwarf mallow, this deep-rooting member of the family Malvaceae grows along waysides, in field borders and on wasteland throughout the Algarve. It is just one of the many kinds of mallows that continue blooming here long after the summer heat has caused most spring wildflowers to shrivel and turn brown.

Broad-leaved Everlasting Pea
(Lathyrus latifolius)
April to June

This scrambling perennial is very common throughout the Algarve, where it can be seen into early summer. The flowers range from pink to purple and sometimes white and, other than being much larger, are very reminiscent of garden sweet peas although lacking the sweet scent for which the garden variety is so valued.

Centaurea pullata
March to June

With its lovely pink-to-purple flowers that hug the ground, this plant is very common in the Iberian Peninsula and is also naturalised in some parts of France. The flowers can be white, although the pink form shown here is far more common in the Algarve.

Algarve Toadflax
(Linaria algarviana)
March and April

Listed as 'vulnerable' in the Red List of plant species, this pretty little wildflower is a fairly common sight in field margins and on waysides in the southern part of the Algarve.

French Lavender
(Lavandula stoechas)
March to June

This is a wildflower to look out for wherever you go in the Algarve. Whether beside the sea or high up in the mountains, French lavender often forms huge plants with numerous flower spikes.

Flaxleaf Pimpernel
(Anagallis monelli)
March to June

Sometimes referred to as shrubby pimpernel, this low-growing wildflower is particularly fond of dry roadside verges, where it does not have to compete with taller vegetation. The flowers are larger than those of the familiar scarlet pimpernel *(Anagallis arvensis)* which is also common in both red and blue forms in the Algarve.

Chicory
(Cichorium intybus)
May to August

Heavenly blue is the best way to describe the colour of these flowers, which are found throughout the Algarve, although they are far less common the further east you travel. Cultivars of this plant tend to have larger flowers. The young leaves are eaten as salad, and the roots when dried form chicory powder which is sometimes added to coffee.

The Spanish oyster plant *(Scolymus hispanicus)* – one of the very few plants that continue blooming despite soaring temperatures in high summer – can often be seen in flower on roadsides from May right through to September

Oleander *(Nerium oleander)* is another plant that withstands the heat of an Algarve summer, and so it is often planted in gardens, on roadside verges and motorway reservations. You will also find oleander growing wild along the banks of rivers and streams.

Coastal Cliffs and Coves

Most holidays in the Algarve focus on the coast and its wonderful coves and beaches. Although the sandy shoreline seldom supports much in the way of plant life, in the coastal strip between the beaches and the towns and villages there are many lovely wildflowers.

Colourful cliff-top walks are one of the many delights of an Algarve seaside holiday.

The cliff tops of the Algarve also provide great habitat for wildflowers and for other wildlife, too. Look out in particular for lizards, swifts, hoopoes and the many other birds that like this kind of terrain, but you will need to take great care when exploring the cliffs as they are being eroded by the constant pounding of the ocean. (It is no coincidence that, despite the magnificent sea views from the cliffs, housing developments are not situated there.)

Wildflowers soften the scars of eroding cliffs near Albufeira.

Catchflies *(Silene colorata)* hug the partial shade of the trees beside a cliff-top walk

The disturbance of feet treading the narrow coastal paths provides just enough cultivation to plant the seeds of shallow-rooting annual wildflowers. Many of the coastal daisies, campions and catchflies are spread in this way on land that would otherwise be covered in perennials of a more thorny nature: good news for the walkers… in more than one sense!

Garrigue habitats

Away from towns and villages, just a short distance back from the sea much of the land is covered with low-growing shrubs and other plants that are, quite literally, pruned by the wind. One of the best examples of this kind of terrain, which is known as garrigue, is at Cape St. Vincent - the most south-westerly point of Europe. The area around the Cape is a National Park (page 65) and the scenery and, in season, the wildflowers are breath-taking.

Wildflowers in the garrigue at Cape St. Vincent

Ophrys lutea, commonly referred to as the yellow ophrys. Often found on wasteland and roadside verges in the Algarve, the yellow ophrys sometimes forms dense colonies, making the most wonderful display in the spring sunshine. This remarkable wildflower is a member of the bee orchid group.

Sea Spurrey
(Spergularia media)
April to August

As its name suggests, sea spurrey is primarily a seaside species, but in the Algarve this low-growing wildflower is also found inland. The picture shows a plant with white flowers, but just as often the flowers are various shades of mauve.

Candytuft
(Iberis species)
April to August

This has long been a garden favourite in the UK, but it grows wild in the Algarve and is nearly always found close to the coast, where it favours limestone hillsides.

Sea Daffodil
(Pancratium maritimum)
July to September

This is one of the few plants to flower late in the season on the Algarve coast. Not only can it withstand the soaring summer temperatures but it is also specially adapted to thrive in the harsh, salt-laden conditions of sandy beaches, which are its primary habitat.

Honeywort
(Cerinthe major)
March to June

This strange-looking plant with its uncurling leaf-and-flower stem can be found near the coast. Cape St. Vincent is a particularly good place for honeywort.

The flowers in this specimen are pale yellow but plants with deep purple flowers also occur.

Yellow-wort
(Blackstonia perfoliata)
April to September

This delicate-looking wildflower has six to eight petals. The flowers, which open only in bright sunlight, can be most frustrating subjects to photograph in countries that are less sunny than Portugal.

Yellow Sea Aster
(Asteriscus maritimus)
March to May

Guaranteed to make you smile when you come across it, this common coastal daisy can be seen throughout the Algarve. It has dark green leaves and bright yellow flowers and often creates dense patches of brilliant colour in the most arid of conditions.

Kidney Vetch
(Anthyllis vulneraria)
March to July

Instantly recognisable, this distinctive wildflower is common in the UK and northern Europe, where it is nearly always yellow. In the Algarve it often has red buds that turn into pink or white flowers.

Sea Rose
(Armeria pungens)
April to July

Also known as the love plant and, less endearingly, as spiny thrift, this beautiful flower is a common sight on stable sand dunes and dry coastal meadows; very occasionally you may find this drought-tolerant plant growing beside cliff-top footpaths.

Common Centaury
(Centaurium erythraea)
May to July

A particularly vigorous plant in the Algarve, although common on the coast common centaury is also frequently found on fallow land and waysides some way inland; it seems ideally suited to the harsh environment and climate of Portugal, often forming large clumps of bright pink flowers that open fully in the sunshine.

Star Clover
(Trifolium stellatum)
March to July

Star clover hugs the ground in coastal areas of the Algarve, although sometimes it can also be found rather further inland in the garrigue.

The five-pointed stars of this unusual-looking flower are sometimes purple rather than pink as in the sample shown here.

Sand Stock
(Malcolmia littorea)
February to May

A member of the cabbage family, Brassicaceae, the range of colours of sand stock are reminiscent of the dolly-mixture sweets so loved by small children. This little plant grows on sandy cliffs throughout the Algarve, and its flowers frequently appear without any suggestion of leaves.

Red Tufted Vetch
(Vicia benghalensis)
April to June

This hairy coastal plant also occurs on fallow farmland away from the coast. The flowers are a deep red and appear in graceful drooping tufts. Nothing like as common or as vigorous as most of the other members of the pea family that occur in the Algarve, red tufted vetch is an exciting find.

Annual larkspur *(Consolida ambigua)* **blooms prolifically in May on the cliff tops above Praia do Marinho, between Carvoeiro and Albufeira.**

In April and May pink pyramidal orchids *(Anacamptis pyramidalis)* make a glorious display on rough ground near the coast – in this instance at Ferragudo.

Agricultural Land

Unlike intensively farmed land, which soon loses most of its native wildlife and flowers, many of the fields, orchards and plantations in the Algarve throng with colourful wildflowers, insects and birds. The main reason is that traditional farming methods are still used extensively in Portugal and therefore most of the land is not subject to an excess of herbicides, pesticides and artificial fertilisers. Regular ploughing and disturbance of the soil is not necessarily a problem for many of the region's wildflowers – indeed, flowers such as the corn poppy thrive as a result. In areas where the soil is less frequently disturbed and only lightly grazed, many of the Algarve's wild orchids can be found.

Friar's cowl *(Arisarum vulgare)* is a perennial that colonises stony fallow fields and pasture land. The flowers of this close relative of the arums appear as early as Christmastime, and most of them are gone by early April.

A fallow field near Aljezur, on the western edge of the Algarve, erupts into a blaze of brightly-coloured wildflowers in springtime.

In sandy and stony land the single-leaved *Scilla monophyllos* blooms from March to May; it is quite common in almond orchards and other lightly-wooded farmland.

The moment the farmer's back is turned, up come those glorious poppies that thrive on disturbed land. Many Algarve cornfields are bright red with poppy flowers throughout spring and early summer.

The dwarf morning glory *Convolvulus tricolor* carpets vast areas of tilled farmland, providing the most spectacular displays from March through to June.

This perennial plant, native to Portugal, thrives in dry sandy soil.

When planted in gardens in northern Europe this attractive wildflower does not survive the winter, unlike the invasive white bindweeds that are the bane of so many gardeners' lives.

35

Christmas visitors to the Algarve are greeted by carpets of Bermuda buttercup, _Oxalis pes-caprae_. These cheery wildflowers are also the most pernicious of weeds in most Mediterranean countries, as they invade every fallow field, golf course and lawn.

Despite its common name, this plant originated in the African Cape and arrived in Portugal around 1825; it is now naturalised throughout the Algarve.

Here Bermuda buttercup makes an old orchard under-planted with broad beans glow golden in the December sunshine.

So many of the later-flowering Algarve plants have tough, prickly or thorny leaves. The thistles go one stage further in their armoury, having prickly flower heads too.

The large blue thistles acting as the guardians of the field boundary (above) are *Onopordum Illyricum*, a species easily distinguished by the downward turned bracts below its flowers.

Like globe artichokes, the flower buds are sometimes cooked and served as a vegetable (after removing the sharp prickly bracts!).

Common asphodel *(Asphodelus aestivus)* often colonises tilled farmland that lies fallow for a year or more. The species name *aestivus* is a reference to summer; however, in the Algarve the first of these stately wildflowers can sometimes be found in bloom at Christmastime, while few if any of the flowers are left by the end of May.

Man orchid *(Aceras anthropophorum)* is an uncommon but wonderful find. This splendid plant is growing on the edge of permanent pasture near Salema.

Several relatives of the familiar (to people from northern Europe) wild garlic occur in the Algarve, and one of the most beautiful is *Allium ampeloprasum*. The specimen shown above was photographed on the edge of a sandy field.

Love-in-a-mist
(Nigella damascena)
April to July

A popular garden plant in the UK and northern Europe, love-in-a-mist grows wild in some parts of the Algarve. Unlike the cultivated varieties, which can be pink, dark blue or lilac, the colours of the wild plants tend to be pale blue and sometimes white.

Spotted Rockrose
(Tuberaria guttata)
February to June

A common sight on the edges of sandy fields, as well as on wasteland, this very variable little plant sometimes produces carpets of flowers. It is a close relative of the various kinds of cistus found in the Algarve region.

Romulea
(Romulea bulbocodium)
March to July

This pretty little flower, which looks very much like a crocus, is in fact a member of the iris family (Iridaceae) and its flowers can vary from almost white to deep lilac. Being such a low-growing plant, it is most often found on rocky ground where it does not have to compete with taller vegetation.

River Valleys, Estuaries and Marshland

Any time from June onwards during the high summer season, visitors to the Algarve could be forgiven for thinking that rivers simply do not exist here. Very little rain falls in the summer, and so the rivers are dependent on winter rainfall. Water abstraction to meet the high demands of the local population, farming and tourism takes its toll, with many rivers dammed and diverted to feed reservoirs. All but the largest rivers become mere trickles by June, making it hard for wetland plants to survive and take a strong hold.

A shrinking stream still supports a brilliant stand of viper's bugloss *(Echium vulgare)* in May. By June a series of disconnected pools is the only sign that a river existed.

Few of the salt-tolerant plants found in the brackish tidal pools and marshland of river estuaries have imposing flowers, but these habitats are of great importance to water birds.

The plants that can survive these harsh and very changeable conditions are highly specialised and have evolved to cope with the salt-laden soil.

Perennial glasswort *(Sarcocornia perennis) in* **the estuary of the River Guadiana at Sapal de Castro Marim Nature Reserve (page 63), on the Portuguese-Spanish border**

In spring the River Arade, near the town of Silves, supports dense mats of water crowfoot, a member of the buttercup family (Ranunculaceae). Already quite shallow by the beginning of May, the river shrinks to a mere trickle in mid-summer.

Arum lilies *(Zantedeschia aethiopica)* have colonised the hollow where a stream flows in winter and early spring. Originally from southern Africa, these flowers (neither true arums nor lilies) are now found in damp, shady places throughout the Algarve.

Pink oxalis *(Oxalis articulata)* is a close relative of the yellow Bermuda buttercup *(Oxalis pres-caprae)* that occurs throughout the Algarve (and indeed of the spring wildflower *Oxalis acetosella,* or wood sorrel, that is found in woodlands throughout northern Europe). Here pink oxalis covers a riverside meadow near Silves.

The paper-white narcissus *(Narcissus papyraceus)* blooms in the early spring along riverbanks, making a splendid display. Regrettably this plant is under threat from some people who seem unable to resist the urge to pick them. They may look good in vases but they have an unpleasant smell and should be left to flower undisturbed.

Mountains and Forests

Before Man's intervention woodland and forests dominated the Algarve landscape. Today trees cover a much smaller area than was the case in the past, and the nature of the woodlands has also changed; however, those Algarve plantations where several species of trees are interspersed and spaced so as to allow light through the canopy still provide rich and varied habitats for a wide range of other flora as well as for wildlife.

Throughout the maquis and up into the higher hills the gum cistus *(Cistus ladanifer)* grows in profusion, the crumpled petals of its flowers often bearing maroon spots. The leaves yield a fragrant oleoresin known as labdanum, which is used in the manufacture of perfumes.

49

Stone pines survive the arid conditions at Felicia Beach. In early spring many wildflowers can be seen blooming in the dappled sunlight beneath these trees.

Down by the coast most wooded land is dominated by the native stone pines *(Pinus pinea)*, from which we get edible pine nuts. This 'lollipop' tree, also known as the umbrella pine, is much loved by those developing golf courses on the sandy coastal strip, because it copes so well with the dry conditions found there.

Acacia trees, also commonly referred to as mimosa, are not restricted to gardens; many have found their way into field hedges, too. The golden racemes of spherical flowers (inset) release a sweet heady odour into the warming February air.

Gum Arabic, once used in adhesives and still in use in confectionary, comes from *Acacia senegal*.

An almond tree bursting into bloom on Christmas Day near Carvoeiro

Almonds and olives were once major exports from Portugal, and there are still places – the area around São Brás de Alportel is one such - where almonds in particular are important crops. With the rapid growth of almond production in California, Portugal's contribution to world output has now fallen to barely one per cent and orchards in more difficult to manage hilly terrain have been abandoned as efforts are concentrated on more productive land. As a result, in some parts of the Algarve you will see almond trees that are no longer harvested; often their fruits (called drupes) have bitter kernels that contain dangerous cyanide toxins.

Almond blossom adds a welcome splash of colour to the landscape in January and February.

Originally a migrant from America, the monarch butterfly now breeds in the Algarve; it loves almond blossom!

The wonderfully contorted trunk of this ancient olive tree, near Ferragudo, bears testimony to its great antiquity.

Olive culture began on the Mediterranean coasts of Lebanon and Palestine more than 7000 years ago. From there, the custom soon spread throughout northern Africa and southern Europe, including the Iberian Peninsula. Olive production quickly became, and in many places remains to this day, an important sector of the Algarve economy.

The flowers beneath this old olive tree are Bermuda buttercups (see page 36), which paint Algarve fields and wasteland bright yellow at the turn of the New Year and on into early spring.

This majestic cork oak tree adorns an otherwise featureless hillside near Silves.

Another native tree that is widely planted throughout most of Portugal is the cork oak *(Quercus suber)*, and there are managed plantations of this evergreen tree in most upland parts of the Algarve. The bark is removed every nine years and, amazingly, the tree simply sets about producing a replacement bark. Cork is still an important Algarve export.

In the mountains cork oaks are interspersed with non-native eucalyptus trees, which are grown for timber and pulp. These high-value trees can thrive where arable crops fail; and, whereas a Scandinavian conifer may take 50 years to reach optimum harvesting size, a eucalyptus can be ready in less than ten years. But there are serious downsides to the monoculture cash-crop plantations of eucalyptus that now cover some 60 per cent of the Monchique region: the soil becomes degraded, most of the native flora die under a blanket of slow-rotting leaves, and the oily wood and leaves constitute a major fire hazard.

Grown singly as ornamental trees in parks and gardens, eucalyptus can be quite magnificent. The leaves of young saplings are round, while those of mature trees are greatly elongated.

The fuzzy flowers of eucalyptus produce an abundance of nectar, and so they are visited by many pollinating insects including several of the Algarve's most colourful butterflies.

In the cooler mountainous regions wildflowers linger far longer than they do down on the coast. A mountain walk through mixed woodland in summer can provide many floral delights.

Shrubby gromwell (Lithospermum fruticosum) is one of the few ground-cover plants that thrive in eucalyptus forests. In clearings and in the dappled sunlight beneath forest tracks beautiful swallow-tail butterflies feed on the nectar provided by the flowers of this long-blooming evergreen shrub.

Spanish iris *(Iris xiphium)* has colonised this area of cleared woodland on a hilltop near Bordiera. With bright orange patches on its azure-blue flowers, Spanish iris is usually it at its best between late March and mid May.

One of the many wild orchids of the Algarve, the broad-leaved helleborine *(Epipactis helleborine)* is a common sight in wooded areas, where it can often be found bathed in dappled sunlight beside forest footpaths. This elegant plant was photographed in mixed woodland between Monchique and Alferce in late April.

Dipcadi serotinum, often referred to simply as dipcadi, is a curious plant, vaguely resembling a bluebell in form and growing in the same kind of habitat. (Dipcadi is sometimes referred to as the 'brown bluebell.')

From March onwards this member of the hyacinth family can be found blooming on stony ground. Dipcadi is particularly abundant in the hills around Monchique, where it is also to be found beside woodland paths and in clearings.

Because of its dull brownish appearance, dipcadi can be easily overlooked.

On Algarve hillsides too steep for cultivation, sward kept short by grazing goats provides ideal habitat for low-growing wildflowers, including grassland orchids.

On a steep hillside near Salema, as in many other lightly-grazed grassland areas of the Algarve, green-winged orchids *(Anacamptis morio)* still bloom in profusion in early spring. In more northerly parts of Europe these nutrient-sensitive wild orchids are becoming increasingly scarce.

The common name 'green-winged' comes from the greenish veins on the 'hood' formed by the upper petals and sepals of the flower. These veins are immediately obvious on paler specimens of the green-winged orchid (such as the one on the left in this picture) but can be difficult to see on the darker ones.

Even within individual colonies of green-winged orchids the colour range can be considerable, with very pale flowers occurring in close proximity to much darker ones.

Invaders and Wanderers

Many of the flowers found in the wild in the Algarve arrived here from other parts of the world with Mediterranean climates. But we also come across flowers in the wilderness that we instinctively think of as cosseted cultivars. The cross-over between wilderness and gardens has been a two-way process over the centuries, and so here are some of the flowers that can cause more than a bit of head scratching.

Well worth a long uphill hike, this wild Peony *(Paeonia mascula)* in common with other wild peonies is increasingly rare because of people digging them up and moving them to gardens. The specimen shown here was photographed in May in an upland forest, where it enjoys the relatively cool and moist conditions.

Peonies have long been used for (often rather dubious) medicinal purposes, but they are now grown, in Europe at least, almost exclusively for ornament.

Another classic Algarve scene is the villa whose walls are smothered in bougainvillea. Brought in from South America, these lovely, long-flowering climbers have been cultivated to produce flamboyant petal-like bracts in many shades of lilac, purple and red.

How so many exotic flowers made their way to the Algarve is unclear, but some stunningly attractive aliens have spread extensively across cultivated land, and from there some of their seeds have been dispersed by birds and mammals into wilder, more remote places.

The fleshy-leaved black flag *(Ferraria crispa)*, an iris from South Africa, has become naturalised on abandoned farmland and in other stony places throughout the Algarve. Blooming in February and March, the exquisite flowers each last but a single day.

Now thoroughly at home in the Algarve, the Hottentot fig *(Carpobrotus edulis)* originated in the south of Africa. It is now naturalised not only on coastal cliffs (even on the fringes of the salt splash zone) but also on waysides and wasteland as far inland as Monchique.

Despite its succulent nature, the Hottentot fig is well adapted to the hot dry climate of an Algarve summer and readily crowds out less vigorous native plants.

A pink form of Hottetot fig is sometimes seen interspersed with the more common yellow variety.

The specific name *edulis* is a reference to the edible nature of the reddish seeds of this plant, which are sometimes eaten either dried or raw but more commonly used to make jam or syrup.

The strawberry tree *(Arbutus unedo)* has a most exotic appearance, but in fact it is native to Portugal and very common in hilly areas. The fruit, which is much more like a lychee than a strawberry, takes a full year to ripen, and so in spring you can see these evergreen bushes in flower while at the same time bearing ripe fruit.

The specific name *unedo* means 'eat only once.' The fruit is rather inferior to either a strawberry or a lychee; however, a brandy-like alcoholic drink, known in the Algarve as Aguardente de Medronho, is made from the fruits of this evergreen bush.

Gardeners in northern Europe fight against seemingly impossible odds to prevent bindweed from pushing its invasive, fragile roots through hedges and fences and into their precious flowerbeds and vegetable plots. In the Algarve, beautiful bindweeds escape from gardens by clambering over walls to decorate trees and bushes in surrounding areas.

Mallow-leaved bindweed *(Convolvulus althaeoides)* **pours over an Algarve field-boundary wall – a welcome splash of extra colour to delight passers by.**

Ipomoea purpurea (left) is just one of the many hundreds of species covered by the common name morning glory. As the name implies, the flowers open in the morning, when they are pollinated by butterflies, bees and other day-flying insects. The trumpet-shaped flowers fade by midday and die in the afternoon. New flowers open every day throughout spring and early summer.

Nature Parks and Reserves in the Algarve

The majority of the Algarve region enjoys protected status of one form or another for its landscape, wildlife or ecology, but if you want to focus on the most ecologically rich and diverse areas then don't miss the opportunity to visit one or more of the nature reserves.

There are three very extensive nature parks/reserves situated in the Algarve. Next to the Spanish border is the smallest of them, Sapal de Castro Marim Nature Reserve; on the coast south of Faro is the Parque Natural do Rio Formosa; and at the western edge of the Algarve you will find Parque Natural do Sudoeste Alentejano e Costa Vincentina.

Sapal de Castro Marim Nature Reserve

On the estuary of the River Guadiana, this is an important wetland site both for birds and for plants. The reserve comprises salt marshes, salt pans (flat areas of land covered with salt and other minerals) and creeks with brackish water on the river estuary. Apart from a wealth of birdlife there is also a fine selection of aquatic plants, such as perennial glasswort – see page 43 – that are specially adapted to cope with salt marsh habitat.

More than 150 bird species, including storks, avocets and flamingos, appear on this reserve during the year, and with some 400 plant species present it's no surprise that a huge variety of insects, amphibians and reptiles also find all the food that they need.

The reserve has a modern visitor centre and a large car park, and there are gravel-path walkways around the lagoons to help people to get the most out of their visits.

Parque Natural do Rio Formosa

Situated between Faro and Vale do Lobo this nature reserve consists of marshland, freshwater lakes, salt pans and sand dunes that provide sanctuary to a huge range of flora and fauna. The park headquarters, which has a visitor centre, is in Quinta de Marim about 3 km east of Olhão. The centre also has a hostel where it is possible to stay overnight.

The nature park encompasses some 18,000 hectares and provides an excellent stopping off point for migratory birds, including colourful flamingos (left). It is also one of the last places in Europe where chameleons, now close to extinction, can still be found.

Lesser water plantain *(Baldellia ranunculoides)* in the margins of a freshwater lagoon

Two good nature trails providing an introduction to this outstanding area and its plants and wildlife are the São Lourenço and Quinta do Lago Nature Trails. The São Lourenço Trail passes through two different types of wetland habitat, salt marshes and freshwater lagoons, while the Quinta do Lago Trail features both marsh and woodland flora.

Park Natural do Sudoeste Alentejano e Costa Vincentina

Covering more than 70,000 hectares this, the largest of the Algarve nature parks, extends from a point near Salema westwards along the coast to Cape St Vincent and then northwards as far as Odeceixe. Around 750 plants and 200 species of birds have been recorded in the reserve. Without question, this area is the best place to start if you want to see a lot of the wildflowers of the Algarve. (Nearly all of the orchid species featured in this book can be found here as well as many others.)

Wildflowers stretching to the horizon at Cape St Vincent

Cape St Vincent forms part of the nature park, and there in springtime the display of limestone flora is a botanical wonderland. The area around the village of Burgau is particularly attractive; among the many wonderful wildflowers to be seen there are the paper-white narcissus in December and January and the yellow hoop-petticoat daffodil in February and March.

Paper-white narcissus
Narcissus papyraceus

Yellow hoop-petticoat daffodil
Narcissus bulbocodium

65

Who Cares for the Algarve Environment?

Instituto da Conservação da Natureza e da Biodiversidade

The government agency responsible for nature conservation and biodiversity policy, site designation and management in Portugal is the Institute for Nature Conservation and Biodiversity - part of the Ministry for the Environment. ICNB manages the Algarve's protected areas, including nature parks and nature reserves.

ICNB
Rua de Santa Marta, 55
1169 – 230 Lisboa
Tel: (351) 213 507 900
www.icnb.pt

Liga para a Protecção da Natureza

The League for the Protection of Nature, a non-governmental organization founded in 1948, contributes to the protection of Portuguese wildlife and ecology via conservation and research projects as well as lobbying and environmental education work.

LPN
Estrada do Calhariz de Benfica, 187
1500-124 Lisboa
Tel: +351 217 780 097
www.lpn.pt

Several other non-governmental organizations work to protect and promote the natural environment of the Algarve, including Sociedade Portuguesa para o Estudo das Aves (the Portuguese Society for the Study of Birds) – www.spea.pt – and Almargem, a group committed to protecting the culture and environment of the Algarve (www.almargem.org).